Hit The Road!
A Kid's Guide To Flam, Norway

Photography by John D. Weigand
Poetry by Penelope Dyan

Bellissima Publishing, LLC
Jamul, California
www.bellissimapublishing.com

Copyright © 2017 by Penny D. Weigand and John D. Weigand

All rights reserved. No part of this book may be reproduced or transmitted in any form or by any means, electronic or mechanical, including photocopying, recording, or by any other means, or by any information or storage retrieval system, without permission from the publisher.

ISBN 978-1-61477-273-6
First Edition

"Wherever you go, go with all your heart."

Confucius

Hit The Road!
Bellissima Publishing, LLC

Introduction

The name Flam comes from an the Old Norse word flá, which means "plain, flat piece of land." It refers to the flood plains of the Flam River. The village of Flam, since the late 19th century, has been a tourist destination; and there are lot of fun things for kids to see and do once you arrive at this quaint little village where many cruise ships dock. Perhaps the most fun is getting to this little village; and whether you travel by train, boat or car, there are lots of things to see along the way. And once you get to Flam you can shop and explore their small museum and get a real glimpse of Flam's colorful past. Just hit the road or the track or the water, whichever the case may be!

Written by award winning author, attorney and former teacher, Penelope Dyan, and filled with the photography of John D. Weigand, this book is intended to educate and show kids what they can see in Flam, as they practice their reading skills through word repetition, word recognition and rhyme. And for even more learning fun, and to see even more of Flam, Norway, watch the free music video that goes along with this book on Bellissimavideo's YouTube channel.

Hit The Road!
A Kid's Guide To Flam, Norway

Photography by John D. Weigand
Poetry by Penelope Dyan

You are on your way to the fjords,
and you're on the train.
But you will stop at Flam, Norway,
all the same!

So forward you go, clickety clack,
as toward a tunnel in the mountain
you head right down that track!

As you pass some houses
you start to slow,
as down that railroad track you go!

Then you see a lovely site,
a beautiful home painted white.
As out the train window you stare,
you can't help but to wonder,
"Who lives in there?"

You train reaches flam, Norway,
and off the train you go.
Your dad chides your mother
for moving too slow.

You see a souvenir shop,
guarded by a troll with a sword.
Another holds the Norway flag.
(Because it means shopping,
YOUR mom doesn't lag.)

Once inside, you ALL start to shop.
You wonder if Mom will EVER stop.
This place is full of lots of great stuff!
But for YOUR mom (the shopper)
it is NEVER enough!

Then not too VERY far outside,
YOU find a GREAT place to play!
You smile and you run
(ahead of Mom and Dad.)
It's such a fun AND happy Day!

Then in the Flam museum you see
a VERY old sled.
And you just can't get it through
YOUR head.
Did they really use THIS sled
instead of a car?
Then you think to yourself,
"I'll bet THEY didn't go far!"

Then you see a part of an OLD train.
It actually sits on an old track!
Even though it was modern back then,
you're glad you're in THIS time now.
Because through time
you would NOT want to travel back!
(And as you stand there,
you just stare and stare.
And you wonder what they WORE
for underwear!)
Now, you know that's a SILLY thought,
but as to SILLY thoughts,
YOU have a lot!

You see an OLD buckboard
right nearby!
And then TWO milk cans
catch your eye!
And you think to yourself,
"When I go to bed,
dreams of ALL of THESE things,
will fill up my head!"

Then before YOU know it,
you're getting right back on that train,
to travel through the cold terrain.
You tell the troll not to cry.
You say "Hasta la vista!"
And you DON'T say, "Good Bye!"

"A farewell is necessary before we can meet again."

Author Unknown

www.ingramcontent.com/pod-product-compliance
Ingram Content Group UK Ltd.
Pitfield, Milton Keynes, MK11 3LW, UK
UKHW060133240426
12048UKWH00002B/18